A Desert Trek

Mike Herschell

Illustrated by

Peter Bull

Climb into the truck and we'll begin our desert trek.

5

Why did we have to wait all day for our trek?

6

Because it is much cooler in the evening.

The Arizona Desert is very hot during the day. In the morning and evening it is much cooler and at night it can be very cold.

7

8

During the daytime many desert animals
hide from the hot sun in burrows and
under rocks. They come out in the
evening and at night.

These rock formations are made when the wind and sand wear away the soft rock. This leaves the hard rocks standing.

It is a giant cactus. It grows
very slowly and can live for two
hundred and fifty years.

13

14

Let's take a look.

The gila woodpecker makes its nest by carving out a hole in the soft flesh of the giant cactus.

15

16

The roadrunner is a kind of cuckoo. But, unlike other cuckoos, it doesn't lay its eggs in other birds' nests. The roadrunner can fly but it usually runs along the ground.

17

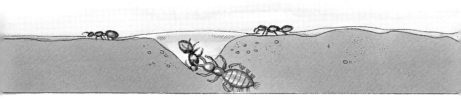

The ant lion is an insect. It digs a little pit in the sand and then buries itself at the bottom. When other small creatures fall into the pit, the ant lion catches them and eats them.

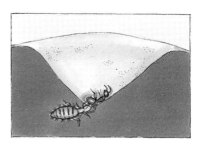

20

The horned lizard is camouflaged so that it looks like the rocks and sand.

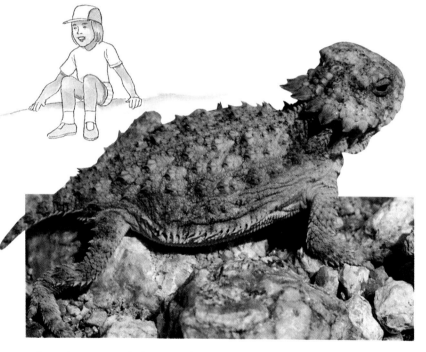

The horned lizard is a reptile, like lots of desert creatures. Its scaly skin stops it drying out in the sun.

Rattlesnakes are shy creatures that hide
away in rocky crevices. They are very
poisonous but will only attack people if
they are disturbed.

24

Kangaroo rats have long back legs,
like kangaroos. They can jump higher
than you!

25

They wake up when we go to bed.

It's your bedtime now and time to go home.

Kit fox

Coyote

27

Look at this picture. How many desert plants and animals do you know? The answers are on the next page, but do not peep until you have tried yourself.

29

The animals and plants in this book are shown at different sizes to their real size. This is how they really look compared to you.

Gila woodpecker

Ant lion

Horned lizard

Kangaroo rat